Restoring America's Travel Brand

A National Strategy to Compete for International Visitors

Recommendations to the
U.S. Secretary of Commerce

From the
U.S. Travel and Tourism Advisory Board

September 5, 2006

Restoring America's Travel Brand

A National Strategy to Compete for International Visitors

TABLE OF CONTENTS

INTRODUCTION:
A NEW GOLDEN AGE OF WORLD TRAVEL

It is safe to say that the world is now entering a new golden age for travel and tourism. A confluence of developments is fueling an era of explosive growth in the world travel market – which is likely to drive a sizable share of the world's future job creation, economic growth and tax revenue. Simply put, travel and tourism, which includes leisure, business, conventions and meetings, educational and medical travel, is one of – if not the most – significant growth industries in the world today.

First, rising disposable income means that vast new markets are joining the world travel community. The market is growing by tens of millions of individuals each year. The number of country-to-country travelers is projected to double within 15 years,[1] and the revenue generated by this business and leisure travel is projected to double within 10 years.[2]

Second, the number of world class travel destinations is proliferating, due to improvements in travel infrastructure and facilities, as well as the easing of restrictions in many parts of the world that were previously inaccessible.

Countries that adapt to these new realities will reap a windfall of new jobs and economic growth.

Third, new technology such as the Internet and mobile communication devices allows for enhanced access to information, greater mobility, and shared cultural experiences on a scale never seen before. Individuals, as well as travel agents, meeting planners and other intermediaries in all corners of the planet are increasingly aware of the expanding array of travel options, and the competition for their business is growing both more intense and more sophisticated.

Within this fast-growing market, consumer expectations, behaviors and booking patterns are also evolving at breakneck speed. Today's world travelers not only originate from more countries, but also more money to spend, an increasing number of worthwhile destinations to choose from, better access to information, and they expect a higher level of service and ease of movement than ever before. In short, they expect nations to *compete* for their business.

Countries that adapt to these new realities will position themselves to reap a windfall of new jobs and economic growth. Those countries that do not, will risk being left behind.

In this paper, the U.S. Travel and Tourism Advisory Board[3] examines the competitive position of the U.S. within the world travel and tourism industry, and recommends a new national strategy to compete for a greater share of this growing market.

---

[1] The U N. World Tourism Organization's *Tourism 2020 Vision* forecasts that international arrivals are expected to reach over 1.56 billion by the year 2020. Of these worldwide arrivals in 2020, 1 2 billion will be intraregional and 0.4 billion will be long-haul travelers.

[2] World Travel and Tourism Council *Progress and Priorities 2006*

[3] The U.S. Travel and Tourism Advisory board consists of 14 industry CEOs, and was formed to advise the Secretary of Commerce on national tourism strategy. The full list of members may be found in the appendix.

THE STATE OF AMERICAN COMPETITIVENESS

Looking solely at the number of – and revenue generated by – visitors to the United States, it is easy to conclude that the U.S. position remains strong. Arrivals to the U.S. – including both trans-border and long-haul travel – are on an upward track, and this year may surpass the record previously set in 2000. This view is also supported by the fact that the U.S. generates far more revenue from international arrivals than any other country in the world.

But a closer analysis reveals troubling indicators that suggest the U.S. competitive position is not nearly as strong as it should be.

At a time when other countries have become better funded, more coordinated and sophisticated in their efforts to attract international visitors, the U.S. still lacks a national strategy to compete. This situation puts the U.S. at a distinct competitive disadvantage in efforts to attract world travel.

The U.S. still lacks a national strategy to compete for world travel

The consequences of this competitive gap have already materialized. A close analysis of key indicators and trend lines reveals that beneath the surface of seemingly good news, the U.S. has been steadily losing market share for years, at a cost of hundreds of billions of dollars and millions of jobs.

Number of Visitors	
The Good:	**The Bad:**
In 2006, the U.S. is projected to return to – and possibly surpass – the levels of international arrivals last reached in 2000.	The U.S. has captured 0% of the nearly 20% growth in country-to-country travel since 2000.[4] By the end of 2005, North America was the *only sub-region of the world to have recorded a decline in arrivals* since 2000[5].

---

[4] U.S. Department of Commerce, U.N. World Tourism Organization
[5] U.N. World Tourism Organization *World Tourism Barometer* January 2006.

Market Share	
The Good:	**The Bad:**
The U.S. captured 6.1% of the 808 million international travelers in 2005 – ranking third behind France and Spain.[6] This represents a second year increase in market share.	U.S. share of international travel has fallen 35% since 1992 – from a high of 9.4% to the current 6.1%. Had the U.S. maintained its share of the world travel market, 27 million more travelers would have visited the U.S. in 2005.[8]
The U.S. captured 12% of the $622 billion in revenue that was spent by country-to-country travelers in 2004 – by far the highest ranking among countries in the world.[7]	U.S. share of revenue from international travel has fallen 29% since 1992 – costing the U.S. an estimated $43 billion in 2005 alone. The cumulative cost since 1992 is estimated at $286 billion in economic growth and millions of jobs.[9] For the cumulative effect on U.S. GDP growth, see the chart below:

Loss of U.S. Marketshare: Effect on GDP Growth

Source: U.S. Department of Commerce Bureau of Economic Analysis

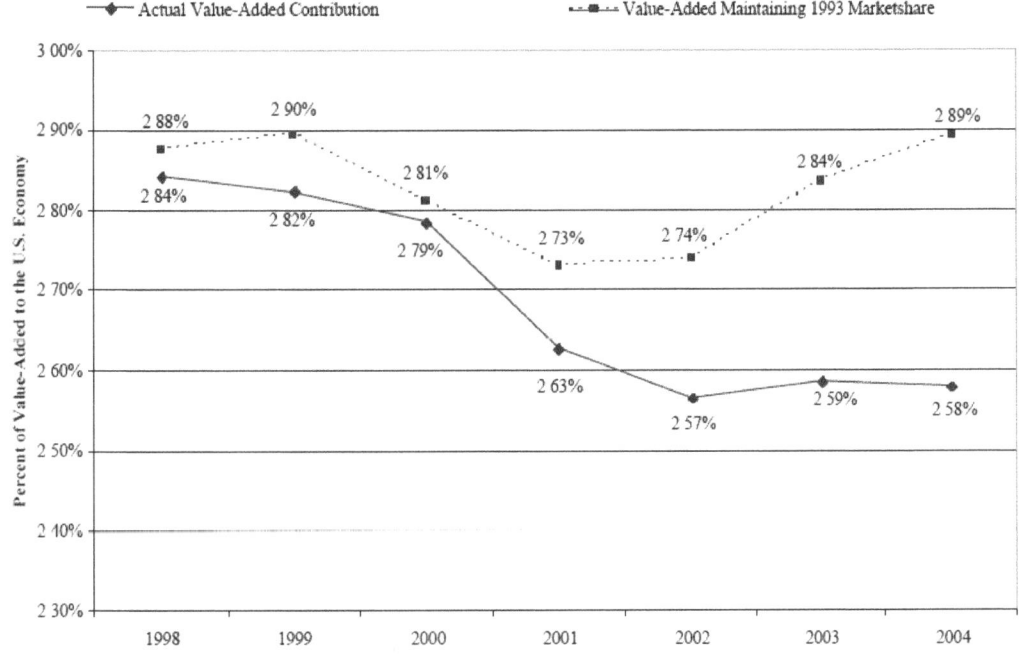

----

[6] U.S. Department of Commerce, Office of Travel and Tourism Industries; U.N. World Tourism Organization
[7] U.S. Department of Commerce, Office of Travel and Tourism Industries; U.N. World Tourism Organization. 2004 is the latest year for which worldwide receipts are available.
[8] U.S. Department of Commerce, U.N. World Tourism Organization
[9] Travel Industry Association estimate.

Revenue	
The Good:	**The Bad:**
The U.S. leads the world in international travel and tourism receipts. The U.S. gained 65% more revenue from international visitors than Spain and 83% more revenue than France.[10]	In 2004 – the most recent year for which world statistics are available – the U.S. took in $8 billion *less* from foreign visitors than it did in 2000, at the same time that total world receipts were $149 billion higher. [11] Meanwhile, lucrative *overseas* travel to the U.S. is still down 16.5% from 2000, with corresponding revenues down 8% in 2005.[12]

Balance of Trade	
The Good:	**The Bad:**
The travel and tourism trade surplus rose to $7.4 billion in 2005, an increase of 84% over 2004 and the second year in a row the surplus has nearly doubled.	Compared to 10 years ago, the U.S. international tourism balance of trade has *declined* nearly 72% – from $26.3 billion in 1996 to $7.4 billion in 2005.[13]

Brand Strength	
The Good:	**The Bad:**
The U.S. benefits from perhaps the widest, richest array of tourism attractions in the world, as well as a world class level of service, infrastructure and hospitality facilities.	The U.S. has fallen from 1st to 6th among dream destinations for international travelers.[14] An international survey of professional travel agents and purchasers showed that 77 percent believed that the U.S. is more difficult to visit than other destinations, while only six percent found it easier.[15]

---

[10] This is due to the fact that the U.S. receives a greater proportion of its visitation from long-haul travelers, who traditionally spend more money than short-haul travelers. On average, international visitors spent just over $1,600 per visitor in the United States, by far the highest level of spending in any country.

[11] U.N. World Tourism Organization. 2004 is the most recent year for which revenue numbers are available.

[12] U.S. Department of Commerce, Office of Travel and Tourism Industries

[13] U.S. Department of Commerce

[14] The Anholt-GMI Nation Brands Index

[15] Travel Industry Association International Travel Survey of 155 international travel buyers, conducted from June 16-June 26, 2006.

THE NEED FOR A NATIONAL STRATEGY

Promoting travel to the United States is in the national interest – in terms of jobs, economic growth and national reputation.

Economic Rewards. Every one percent of world market share that the U.S. regains will result in an estimated 8.1 million more visitors; $13.4 billion in additional revenues; 153,000 additional U.S. jobs; $3.5 billion in additional payroll; and $2 billion in additional tax revenues.[16]

Diplomatic Rewards. The State Department spends more than $800 million on programs designed to communicate America's values to other countries and cultures, through exchange, information programs and other public relations activities. [17]

> *Promoting travel to the United States is in the national interest – in terms of jobs, economic growth and national reputation*

For a fraction of this cost, the travel and tourism industry can be a powerful partner in these efforts. The simple act of ASKING people to visit us – whether through marketing or friendlier borders – will demonstrate to the world that we are an open, welcoming and friendly society.

For these reasons, the U.S. Travel and Tourism Advisory Board offers the following recommendations for a national strategy to gain competitive advantage in the world travel and tourism market.

The Elements of a National Strategy

1. **Make it easier for people to visit, by balancing hospitality with security.** A June 2006 survey of international travel agents and purchasers showed that 77% believe the United States is more difficult to visit than other destinations. This perception creates a significant disadvantage for the U.S. in its efforts to compete for world travelers. Our national strategy must include an entry process that is faster, friendlier, and more efficient.

2. **Ask people to visit us, with a nationally-coordinated marketing program.** The U.S. is one of the few industrialized countries in the world today without a nationally-coordinated program designed to promote its destinations to international travelers. Clearly, the U.S. must implement its own nationally-coordinated marketing campaign in order to be competitive with other countries in the new world market.

3. **Demonstrate the value of travel and tourism.** An effective strategy must be an informed strategy, and it is therefore important to invest in assessing and re-assessing both the industry's competitiveness within the world market, and the success of U.S. investments in promotion and ease of travel.

---

[16] Travel Industry Association of America calculation, using Department of Commerce figures.
[17] The Department of State's FY 2007 Budget Request which shows a request of $351 million for public diplomacy and $474 million for educational and cultural exchanges.

MAKE IT EASIER FOR PEOPLE TO VISIT US
A Report of the Ease of Travel and Public Diplomacy Subcommittee

---

SITUATION ANALYSIS:

In response to the September 11 terrorist attacks, the U.S. government and the travel and tourism industry have made massive investments in securing borders, facilities and infrastructure. The industry is proud of its partnership with the government in these efforts. However, the many steps the government has taken to exclude potential terrorists, while supported by the travel and tourism industry, regrettably may have created the impression that the United States does not welcome international visitors. In the process of focusing exclusively on security, the U.S. has become less competitive than other countries because the perception has been created that it is more difficult and more costly to travel to the U.S. than elsewhere. The collective expertise of the industry and surveys show that many legitimate potential international visitors now deliberately avoid travel to the U.S. due to real and perceived barriers to entry. U.S. businesses often find it difficult to bring and attract people to the U.S. for training, meetings, conferences and other business activities.[18]

A survey of international travel professionals showed that 77 percent believed that the United States was more difficult to visit than other destinations

While the U.S. has focused on the necessary work of border security with minimal consideration to facilitation matters, other countries have invested in competing for the international traveler, both through direct advertising and promotions[19] and through coordinated government policies aimed at attracting investment in tourism and travelers themselves. These policies include offering visas without charge or permitting visa-free travel[20] as well as coordinating government and private sector actions in order to attract international visitors.

The Department of Commerce's Travel Barometer reports, which survey international travel professionals, support our concerns about U.S. government procedures and insufficient communications as barriers to inbound travel. The recent UK Barometer notes that:

---

[18] The letters of Mr. J.W. Marriott, Jr , Chairman of the President's Export Council of December 6, 2005 and September 29, 2004 to the President discuss this subject at length.

[19] Australia announced in 2005 that it would spend more than $300 million on international tourism promotion over three years, focused on the U.K, Japan, China and India. Singapore has budgeted $190 million over five years for tourism promotion, while Hong Kong's 2005 budget was $64 million over two years, most of which was directed to global publicity and promotion programs (all figures in U.S. dollars). These figures dwarf U.S. federal government expenditures on tourism promotion both in absolute and per-capita terms ($5.00-$9.00 annually per capita for those three countries, compared to about one cent per capita in the United States). 20 Canada, for example, permits Korean and Mexican citizens visa-free entry and charges $55 for a single-entry visa (vs. $100 for the United States) and allows a family visa rate that is not available in the United States. Australia's electronic travel authorization visa system is automated, generally free and returns a reply almost instantly, while France charges about $45 for a short-term visa.

Starting in 2004, entrance procedure to the U.S. consistently has registered as the top barrier for travel. These barriers included the following factors: misinformation for consumers on entry and exit requirements to the USA, actual entrance procedures to visit the USA, visa processing time. Two-in-three program participants consider misinformation for consumers on entry and exit requirements as a travel barrier.[21]

The Barometer reports from Germany and Mexico echo the themes of difficult entry procedures and poor communications as barriers.

A June 2006 survey completed by155 international travel professionals throughout the world showed that 60 percent reported clients were concerned or confused about rules and procedures regarding international travel to the U.S. A separate survey question showed that 77 percent believed that the U.S. was more difficult to visit than other destinations, while only six percent found it easier and 18 percent said "about the same." Respondents repeatedly cited visa requirements, "hassle," price, and the perception that the U.S. was unwelcoming as the reasons that customers chose destinations in other countries.[22]

The following recommendations are designed to address current gaps and deficiencies in U.S. competitiveness in ease of travel, and help restore the U.S. as the world's premier international travel destination.

I.   Remove Unnecessary Barriers to Travel

II.   Create a Welcoming First Impression

III. Provide Stronger Voice for Travel and Tourism in Government

IV.   Avoid Inappropriate Taxes, Fees and Regulations

---

[21] UK , Germany and Mexico Travel Barometers, May 2006 Update. U.S. Department of Commerce.
[22] Travel Industry Association International Travel Survey. The survey was held from June 16, 2006- June 26, 2006. 155 completed responses were received during that period.

I. Remove Unnecessary Barriers to Travel

These suggestions are intended to ensure that the U.S. reduces barriers to inbound travel, effectively communicates with the prospective visitor and reduce taxes, fees and regulations that target travel and tourism. A successful effort promises to contribute to the image of the U.S. abroad and to the U.S. economy across many sectors. Each subcategory identifies an area in which the U.S. is currently not as competitive as other countries in facilitating legitimate inbound international visitors and provides recommendations to help redress this imbalance.

1. **Reduce Disruption Threatened by Implementation of the Western Hemisphere Travel Initiative (WHTI).** The WHTI is meant to improve the security of U.S. borders by adopting consistent standards for identity documents. It imposes new requirements for national identity documents on citizens of Western Hemisphere countries, and also applies to U.S. citizens re-entering the U.S.. Unfortunately, relatively short deadlines and failure to communicate with the traveling public has put WHTI in a position to disrupt vital trans-border travel. Travel and tourism will also be greatly affected in states far from the physical border: Florida, California and Nevada have the largest inbound markets for Canadians in terms of spending. A recent survey showed that half of Canadians would go to the U.S. less often or not at all if required to present a passport or other identification at the border.[23] The TTAB therefore urges the Secretary to play a role in reducing the disruption by seeking the following actions:
   - Extend the WHTI deadline by at least 18 months until proven technology standards are agreed upon and implemented and a uniform low-cost alternative to passports are ready for use by all travelers whether by land or sea. As of June 30, 2006 the Senate Appropriations Committee had approved an amendment that would delay implementation of the WHTI until June 1, 2009. We urge the Secretary to support this amendment.
   - Make the alternative to the U.S. passport (known as "PASS") under consideration for land border use also available to air and sea travelers.
   - As the requirements affecting land borders threaten extensive travel disruptions along the Canadian land border, we strongly recommend that the U.S. government immediately begin to work in partnership with Canadian officials to ensure that travelers on both sides of the border are educated about WHTI requirements and have the proper documentation by the deadline.
   - Work with the U.S. Departments of State and Homeland Security to develop and execute a massive communications campaign, in partnership with the private sector, to get the message out about the new requirements.

2. **Facilitate Issuance of Non-immigrant (Visitor) Visas (NIVs) to Legitimate Travelers.** The cost and inconvenience of applying for a U.S. visa is clearly a barrier to inbound travel. Many other countries that compete for visitors have no visa

---

23 2006 Survey of 1,500 Canadian citizens by Leger Marketing made available to the press.

requirements or, as in the case of Australia, have a very quick and efficient method for issuing travel authorization. Inbound travel by foreign residents is a U.S. export; the fact that the U.S. is not competitive in the non-immigrant visa function is therefore a self-imposed trade barrier.[24] The travel and tourism industry and the U.S. economy lose when prospective visitors decide not to visit the U.S. due to lengthy waits for visa interviews, prohibitive costs and the sometimes extreme distances visa applicants must travel, causing inordinate additional trip costs just to visit the U.S.

<u>Visa Staffing and Waits: the Current Competitive Situation.</u> The U.S. Department of State, its Visa Office in Washington D.C. and Consular Officers throughout the world have performed a remarkable job in recent years in implementing a host of new security requirements, including the near-100 percent interview requirement for NIV applicants and the requirement to obtain a fingerprint impression from such applicants. The addition of over 500 officers in NIV sections outside of the U.S. is a welcome step forward.

Despite this progress, the NIV function remains chronically understaffed and underfunded relative to the critical role it plays at the frontline of the U.S. public image abroad and to facilitating inbound travel to the U.S. A recent U.S. Government Accountability Office (GAO) report notes that almost half of State's 211 visa-issuing posts reported maximum wait times for visa interviews of 30 or more days and that interview waits were 30 plus days every month at 20 posts. In the same report the GAO reiterated its 2002 and 2005 recommendations that State reassess and prepare a plan to address consular staffing requirements.

We draw attention in particular to the long waits required to obtain a visa interview in Brazil,[25] China, India, Mexico and Venezuela as continuing serious impediments to international inbound travel and tourism. Permanent rationing of access to visas is contrary to facilitating inbound travel and tourism and to public diplomacy goals.

<u>Improve Overseas Visa Facilities.</u> Funding for expanding and improving visa facilities or constructing new facilities overseas is virtually nonexistent.[26] Advertising and promotion cannot overcome the negative publicity the U.S. receives daily in countries where waits for visa interviews are long and facilities are cramped and uncomfortable for prospective visitors and consular staff. We therefore urge greater funding for expanding, improving and opening new NIV facilities and have tentatively identified China, Brazil and India as those countries in particular need of new NIV facilities. We also suggest that the Department of State consider whether existing facilities not currently used for visa issuance could be adapted for that function.

---

[24] A June 2006 survey of 155 international travel professionals by the Travel Industry Association showed that long waits, cost of visas and distance required to apply for visas were visa applicants' major complaints.

25 A 1998 GAO report shows Brazil has long suffered from visa backlogs. "Tourist Visa Processing Backlogs Persist at U.S. Consulates," GAO March 1998 pp 2.

[26] In FY 2003 and 2004 State obligated just $10.2 million to 79 consular workspace improvement projects at 68 posts. A GAO report found that even these meager funds were used for temporary solutions at locations awaiting new embassy space. United States Government Accountability Office, "Border Security; Reassessment of Consular Resource Requirements Could Help Address Visa Delays" April 4, 2006. pp 11.

<u>Ensure Effective Program Management for the $700 Million Plus Visa Function.</u> We highlight that visa fees (known as machine readable visa fees) generate significant revenues for the U.S. government and the Department of State. Using State's own figures for annual NIV applications of about 7 million multiplied by the $100 machine-readable visa (MRV) application fee (and excluding all other visa-related fees), MRV fees alone generate $700 million annually, or well over half of State's FY 2007 budget of $1.14 billion for the whole of the Border Security Program. While State retains only a portion of visa revenues, the size, revenue and importance of the visa function demands greater investment in technology, coordination among government agencies and experienced managerial oversight.

<u>The Industry's Offer.</u> The travel and tourism industry is ready to partner with the Departments of State and Homeland Security to improve the visa application process and the arrivals experience in a manner that does not compromise security. Through the Travel Business Roundtable and the TIA, the travel industry is also prepared to assist in highlighting the importance of the travel industry to the U.S. economy and providing or designing supplementary customer service training for consular officers and border agents if so desired. We welcome the opening of new Business Visa Centers and the new emphasis on expediting issuance of B-1 (business) visas. Innovations promised in the Rice-Chertoff Joint Vision (RCJV), such as electronic NIV applications and the planned pilot program for remote NIV interviews through video link, are all steps toward making the process more technologically advanced and therefore less burdensome.

<u>Specific Recommendations Regarding Visitor Visa Policies.</u> We recommend that the Secretary of Commerce seek ways to suggest that the Department of State consider:

- Expanded training for consular officers regarding the importance of travel facilitation and making customer service a part of consular officers' review process;
- Finding ways to quickly reduce consular delays by using technology and more appropriately allocating staff across shifts, working hours, and peak demand seasons;
- Establishing benchmarks for visa wait times, focusing on the delay in obtaining an interview;
- Expanding Business Visa Centers to all 211 visa processing posts worldwide;
- Eliminating the archaic "I" journalist visa designation;[27]
- Creating a communications campaign highlighting the openness of the U.S. and ensuring that senior State officials include this message in their public presentations;
- Re-negotiating visa reciprocity schedules, which unnecessarily limit the duration of visas that the U.S. offers;

---

[27] Eliminating the "I" visa category, which requires journalists who could otherwise travel under the visa waiver program to apply for a visa promises to improve the image of the United States among foreign journalists and to minimally reduce workload in visa sections abroad.

- If permitted, reestablish a program that allows those working in the U.S. to renew NIVs without leaving the U.S. in order to reduce the burden on consular resources and improve service to legitimate visa applicants;
- Exploring with Congress whether the personal interview requirement could be waived in appropriate, low risk cases, perhaps with fingerprint capture at the Port of Entry or a remote location;
- Actively seeking a way to eliminate the personal interview requirement for those who have previously provided a biometric indicator and have consistently visited the U.S.; and
- Implementing in all NIV sections the best practices currently in place in certain sections, including:
    - Establishing a "Business Window" at posts, and setting aside time-blocks for business visas
    - Permitting group NIV appointments; and
    - Utilizing business facilitation units.[28]

3. **Maintain and Expand the Visa Waiver Program.** The Visa Waiver Program (VWP) is central to keeping the U.S. competitive for inbound international travel; more than 2/3 of all overseas travelers enter the U.S. under the VWP. Twenty-seven countries' passport holders benefit from the freedom to enter the U.S. without previously applying for short-term visitor visas. New measures to enhance the security of passports themselves, the U.S. VISIT entry-exit system and other processes make visa-free travel to the U.S. more secure than ever. The industry continues to strongly support the VWP and we encourage the U.S. government to expedite entry into the program of every country that qualifies. Further, countries need to know exactly what they need to do to be granted VWP status. VWP applicants are required to achieve a certain set of criteria, yet in some cases, officials from other countries have complained that the U.S. government agencies have not communicated in a clear fashion what these requirements are.

4. **Build on the Success of U.S. VISIT.** We highlight the success of the U.S. VISIT program as an example of effective industry-government cooperation that has enhanced border security with minimal disruption to international visitors. It also acknowledges some remaining challenges, such as full implementation of exit processes and transition from two to ten finger scans and proposed expansion of the program to include additional classes of visitors, including U.S. Lawful Permanent Residents and many Canadian citizens. We look forward to continued public-private sector cooperation to help meet these challenges.

5. **Address Barriers to Air Travel.** Commercial airlines are proud of their investment in technology and procedures to serve security and other government goals. Regrettably, U.S. government agencies have frequently failed to make the investment in technology, customer service and rationalization of forms and procedures to allow

---

[28] Discussed in State Cable 225608 of October 10, 2004.

that investment to pay off for the industry, the traveler and the U.S. economy.
Examples include:

- Absence of sustained agency coordination of domestic and international air passenger prescreening programs;
- Lack of robust data sharing among U.S. government agencies and between the U.S. and other governments, which has led to duplicative and redundant airline passenger data collection and resulting passenger disservice;
- Continued suspension of the Transit Without Visa program, which had facilitated international travel through the U.S. and attracted international service to U.S. airports;
- Threatened massive delays of all international flights to permit CBP to process passenger data provided by airlines (so called "APIS –60");
- Failure to provide funding to airlines for the proposed APIS Quick Query (AQQ) pilot program, which is meant to ensure timely departures of international flights now threatened under the APIS-60 concept;
- Discouraging international carriers from serving U.S. airports by uncompetitive execution of security procedures for flights transiting the U.S.;[29]
- U.S. government agency reluctance to eliminate redundant and outdated paper forms and processes leading to needless inconveniences for arriving passengers. The continued requirement that international visitors complete the paper I-94 form despite the fact that the same biographic information is collected electronically through APIS procedures is one example of this problem.

The list of barriers to air travel and inconveniences faced by air travelers demand that the involved agencies consult with industry, rationalize procedures and fully invest in technology. The Board therefore suggests that the Secretary use his influence to identify these failures as barriers to trade and press the responsible agencies to address them.

---

29 As just one recent example, Air New Zealand confirmed in April 2006 that it was abandoning Los Angeles as the stopover on its London-Auckland service due to passenger complaints about security checks at Los Angeles airport. It will move that service over Hong Kong in October. (The Telegraph, "Sunshine State Loses its Allure for Britons," April 8, 2006).

II. Create a Welcoming First Impression

While surveys have not been conducted to establish the precise drivers of the recent decline in U.S. reputation, there is evidence to suggest that negative perceptions driven by the real and perceived experience at our borders may play a significant role.[30] Marketing experts understand that the most powerful driver of reputation is word-of-mouth. Any effort to improve the U.S. image in the world must include a thorough assessment of the first impression that visitors form as they enter the U.S., followed by a concerted effort to balance necessary security measures with an equal investment in friendliness and efficiency. Visitors should come away from their first contact with the U.S. feeling that they received a warm welcome.

1. **Staff Federal Inspection Services (FISs) and TSA Fully and Efficiently.** The first contact that many arriving international visitors have with the U.S. is with Federal Inspection Services, most notably Customs and Border Protection (CBP) and the Transportation Security Administration (TSA). There is wide consensus that staffing of at least some FISs and TSA inspection points does not adequately meet demand. Slow entry into the U.S. and delays due to TSA's re-screening stand in stark contrast to efficient procedures in many other countries.[31] Canada and the Netherlands are two examples of countries that have prioritized efficient inspections and air transit services and have succeeded in attracting international air service and passengers disproportionate to their populations.

   Expedite Model Ports of Entry. We emphasize the importance of the Model Ports of Entry (MPOE) element of the Rice-Chertoff Joint Vision (RCJV), which is intended to identify and implement best practices at airports with a large volume of international arriving passengers. United Airlines is involved in the project at Washington Dulles. Full and efficient staffing of FIS facilities in pilot cities, other U.S. ports of entry and U.S. preclearance facilities outside of the country is essential to improving the efficiency and friendliness by which the U.S. processes inbound international travelers.

   Develop Metrics to Evaluate Staffing Patterns. The Model Ports of Entry (MPOE) project should begin by developing appropriate metrics to evaluate staffing and operations at the MPOEs. We also reiterate the offer of industry expertise in staffing patterns to the FISs. Most importantly, we stand ready to work actively with the Secretary to seek full and efficient FIS and TSA staffing at air, sea and land ports.

---

[30] Commerce Foreign Commercial Service officers responded to a survey of impediments to travel to the United States of which 4 identified (mis) treatment of visitors as an impediment to inbound travel. The response from Germany noted, "It is perceived that foreign visitors are unwelcome and we have heard complaints about travelers being treated in the same way as criminals (with fingerprinting and digital photos.)" Many commented that the DHS immigration officers were friendlier on their last visit to the U.S." "Travel Impediments as Reported by Foreign Commercial Service Offices of the U.S. Department of Commerce" May 2006.
[31] Air New Zealand confirmed in April 2006 that it was abandoning Los Angeles as the stopover on its London-Auckland service due to passenger complaints about security checks at Los Angeles airport. It will move that service over Hong Kong in October. (The Telegraph, April 8, 2006, "Sunshine State Loses its Allure for Britons.")

<u>Leverage Industry Expertise.</u> Members of the Board and other industry participants have already offered their expertise in management of line waits and staffing patterns to the FISs. The TIA has begun discussions with the Under Secretary of State for Public Diplomacy and Public Affairs and remains committed to providing travel industry professionals to assist CBP in developing more flexible queuing strategies. The industry is also waiting for the government's cue to advise FISs on signage and the use of international symbols to direct travelers and prepare them for the inspection process.

Several leading travel companies are willing to loan customer service/hospitality experts who could provide training for CBP officers at the Federal Law Enforcement Training Center in Georgia. Such training could complement CBP officers' vital law enforcement work with training on optimal methods for welcoming visitors to the U.S.

2. **Incorporate Hospitality Within DHS Goals and Performance Review Process.** Many of our recommendations are based on the importance of the efficient functioning of the Department of Homeland Security (DHS). It will be difficult to achieve these goals if DHS does not establish a mechanism within its performance review process that accounts for the needs of the legitimate traveler and the travel and tourism industry in decision-making, goals, resource allocation and employee evaluation.

3. **Better Coordinate Security Requirements with Other Governments.** In recent years, lack of coordination and communication as well as inconsistent standards between the U.S. and other governments have threatened the efficient and free-flow of international travelers into the U.S. and damaged the reputation of the U.S. as a destination. More such threats are on the horizon. A renewed U.S. government commitment to consultation and coordination with other governments, especially regarding security and privacy is critical.

Such coordination between governments facilitates not just international inbound travel, but also international-to-domestic travel and encourages use of the U.S. and its airlines and airports for 3rd country to 3rd country travel. We therefore suggest that the Secretary and his counterparts at DHS, the Department of State and the Department of Transportation (DOT) direct their staff to actively coordinate activities that affect international travel with their equivalents in other governments.[32] Seeking avenues to eliminate TSA re-screening of international arriving baggage transferred to onward flights is an obvious initial goal.

4. **Provide a Warm Welcome to Arriving International Visitors.** With this goal, the travel industry has offered its services through the Department of State in producing professionally designed "welcome" videos that would play on a loop on flat panel

---

[32] The lengthy negotiations between CBP and the European Commission regarding CBP access to airline passenger data (passenger name records, or PNRs) is an example of the type of involved negotiations required to ensure that U.S. government requirements are consistent with international requirements and do not impede international inbound travel.

monitors in the international arrivals hall of selected airports. These videos might present welcome messages and instructions, and permit the FISs to deliver timely information to arriving international travelers.

5. **Ensure Accurate and Timely U.S. Government Communications Regarding Travel Requirements.** The plethora of new travel requirements the U.S. has imposed on foreign visitors in recent years has rarely been supported by strong communications from the U.S. government. While the industry continues to be ready to highlight official communications to the traveling public it cannot serve as a substitute for effective direct communications between the U.S. government and the traveling public. As mentioned earlier, Commerce's own Barometer reports underscore the fact that official communications about entry requirements have been substandard and therefore create confusion that discourages travel. The uncertainty created by last-minute decisions and inadequate communications regarding the biometric passport requirement dampened demand for travel and increased negative perceptions of the U.S. We suggest that a true, well-funded communications plan must be an integral part of implementing any new entry or exit requirement, including any expansion of U.S.-VISIT. The industry stands ready to lend its expertise to U.S. agencies in this regard.

III. Provide Stronger Voice for Travel and Tourism in Government

When government officials and agencies speak for security, who in government is charged with speaking for travel and tourism? It is clear that other countries that compete with the U.S. have coordinated visa/entry/exit, air service, regulatory, tax and other policies that favor travel and tourism as well as meaningful budgets for traditional promotional campaigns to attract these visitors. Countries that are competitive for tourism also ordinarily have ministries of tourism or other governmental entities that help coordinate policy decisions that impact this sector. The U.S., by contrast, has no specific Ministry of Tourism or Office high enough to advocate these issues at the highest policy levels in support of this vital, growing sector.

1. **Create an Elevated Voice for Travel and Tourism Within Government**.
Since the U.S. Travel and Tourism Administration was dismantled in 1996, the travel and tourism industry has suffered from the absence of a dedicated high-ranking office in the Federal government designed to enhance the industry's role in creating jobs and economic growth. While the Office of Travel and Tourism Industries has served a valuable role in providing research and expertise on the industry, and has served effectively in the international organizations for government policy deliberations and representation, a dedicated higher-ranking office with the power to coordinate government policy to enhance the nation's competitive standing in the global travel market is sorely needed. This office should be designed to accomplish the following:
   - Serve as an institutional home and voice for the industry;
   - Energize the interagency process regarding travel and tourism through an elevated Tourism Policy Council with ex-officio status for private sector representation. All government decisions that potentially affect this industry should receive early attention in the interagency process;
   - Identify existing private sector advisory committees, ensure that they include the right representatives from the industry and see that their recommendations are widely shared across agencies and with other private sector groups and the public; and
   - Coordinate the roles of other government agencies to more effectively expand travel and tourism promotion, product development and infrastructure needs and development.

   Ideally, this office would help to coordinate the implementation of many of the recommendations contained in this paper.

2. **Enhance Coordination Between Federal Agencies, Local Government and Private Sector.** We commend the Secretary for his steadfast dedication to elevating the role of travel and tourism within the Bush Administration. While his leadership is central and critical to advancing our policy goals, the recommendations within this document reflect the diversity of our industry issues and their diffuseness among many Cabinet Departments. Many of these issues

fall outsideof the Commerce Department's jurisdiction, including at least some elements of visa policy, public diplomacy, immigration reform, transportation policy and homeland security concerns. In addition, America's mayors and governors have long been on the cutting edge of creative travel and tourism policy. We believe that close coordination among Cabinet Departments with the nation's mayors, governors and private sector interests are all necessary if our industry is to receive the policy consideration it deserves. The successful implementation of the Board's policy recommendations are predicated upon the ability of the federal government to functionally process and execute them.

2. **Create a Private Sector Stakeholders Committee on Visa Matters.** We second the U.S. Chamber of Commerce's recommendation to create an advisory committee of private sector stakeholders that would advise the Departments of State and Homeland Security on visa matters. This suggested committee would be intended to develop cooperative solutions to the visa matters that are key barriers to travel.[33]

3. **Identify Causes Behind Shifts in Travel Away from the U.S.** We suggest that the Department of Commerce identify key countries where international travel has shifted away from the U.S., and determine the causes behind these shifts in travel. Identifying and quantifying travel diversion is the first step towards regaining market share, either through reducing barriers to U.S. exports of travel services or though other means.[34] We welcome the insights available in the Barometer reports and in the Department's recent survey of Foreign Commercial Service (FCS) employees abroad about barriers to inbound travel[35] and we expect that these reports are circulated to State and DHS to inform their efforts.

4. **Fund, Staff and Establish Goals and Metrics for the Rice-Chertoff Joint Vision**. We welcome the intentions of Rice-Chertoff Joint Vision (RCJV), which Secretaries Rice and Chertoff announced in early 2006. The RCJV's goals of easing travel barriers to the U.S. and of improving the U.S. image abroad are congruent with the travel industry's goals, and many of our recommendations could be implemented through the RCJV.

U.S. Departments of State and Homeland Security officials responsible for the initiative briefed Subcommittee staff on progress in the project's first five months. During this period the RCJV seems not to have established concrete goals beyond the normal plans of the agencies nor is it clear that it has any timelines or metrics by which to judge its success. Further, the RCJV has no permanent staff and does

---

33 Statement of the U.S. COC to the House Committee on Government Reform, April 4, 2006.

34 A 2005 study of South Koreans' international travel patterns by the Korea Visit USA Committee Commerce illustrates that with the advent of stricter in-person visa interview rules and resulting long waits for interviews in recent years, Korean travel has shifted away from the United States to destinations with minimal entry requirements.

35 15 Commerce FCS officers responded to this survey of which 4 identified (mis) treatment of visitors as an impediment to inbound travel. The response from Germany noted, "It is perceived that foreign visitors are unwelcome and we have heard complaints about travelers being treated in the same way as criminals (with fingerprinting and digital photos.) Many commented that the DHS immigration officers were friendlier on their last visit to the U.S." "Travel Impediments as Reported by Foreign Commercial Service Offices of the U.S. Department of Commerce." May 2006.

not have its own budget. We strongly recommend that Secretaries Rice and Chertoff move quickly to seek the private sector's input in establishing concrete goals, timelines and associated budgets needed to reach those objectives

IV. Avoid Inappropriate Taxes, Fees and Regulations

Federal, state, local, special entity and foreign-government imposed taxes and fees on rental cars, commercial aviation, hotels and restaurant meals, among other services increase the cost of travel and can dampen demand for inbound travel. Much of this tax burden placed on travelers is used to fund programs may be of general public benefit – but have no clear connection or benefit to the industry or consumers being taxed. Government programs that benefit the public at large should not be funded by travel-specific taxes and fees; any taxes and fees directed at travel and tourism should have a clear connection to and benefit those paying the taxes.

In the case of rental cars, special excise taxes fund 18 sports and venue projects and additional such taxes are under consideration. Despite the billions of dollars paid by rental car companies and customers in excess of normal sales taxes there is no special benefit to rental car customers from such special venue taxes nor is there a direct connection between renting a car and using the public facilities or programs the taxes fund. In the case of commercial air transportation, international passengers pay eight types of taxes and fees to the U.S. government in addition to sales taxes, including fees that subsidize security, which is properly a national priority. Air and rental car transportation is not a luxury that should be taxed as such. The fact that other modes of transportation, such as bus and rail are not similarly taxed illustrates this fact. Hotel and restaurant taxes and taxes and fees directed at other aspects of the travel and tourism industry are sometimes similarly overused to fund programs that should be general obligations.

1. **Discourage Inappropriate Taxes and Fees.** In light of the misuse of taxes and fees on travel and tourism at all levels of government, we emphasize that some existing types of taxes for the broad public benefit inappropriately target travel and tourism, thus decreasing the international competitiveness of the U.S. as a destination. We urge the Department of Commerce to work on ways to discourage such discriminatory taxing structures and ask that the Department of Commerce work in the interagency process to discourage travel taxes imposed by international authorities when the revenue raised has no clear benefit or connection to the travel and tourism industry. We also suggest a Commerce study of taxes and fees related to travel across countries in order to help determine the U.S. competitive position in this regard.

2. **Review CBP Rates.** We seek the assistance of the Department of Commerce in reiterating the airline industry's call for a thorough review of CBP rates and charges based on costs.[36] Any further increase in government fees on arriving international passengers directly threatens the goal of attracting international visitors to the U.S.

---

[36] CBP charges each arriving international passenger a user fee that covers CBP inspections costs. This request for review is particularly urgent given CBP's April 2006 proposal to raise inspections fees across the board. The commercial airline industry has long believed that CBP fees levied on commercial passengers are unjustly high and that these fees subsidize other CBP functions.

3. **Head Off Regulatory and Indirect Barriers to Travel**. In addition to direct taxes and fees, mandates from government agencies that target travel and tourism can hamper the goal of facilitating inbound travel. As an illustration, the U.S. Centers for Disease Control's (CDC) recent Notice of Proposed Rulemaking would require cruise lines and airlines to collect massive new amounts of personal data from passengers at a direct cost of up to $800 million annually. No other country imposes the cost of public health directly on the travel industry. As another recent example this year the Department of Transportation proposed to require airlines to provide oxygen free of cost to any passenger upon request, regardless of demonstrated medical need. Complying with this rule, if made final, would raise costs to airlines, dampen demand and possibly make some air service uneconomical. In these and similar matters, we urge the Secretary of Commerce to actively engage in the interagency process with a view to protecting the travel and tourism industries from these and other regulatory threats.

ASK PEOPLE TO VISIT US:
A Report of the Promotion Subcommittee

SITUATION ANALYSIS:

The United States is one of the only industrialized countries in the world today that lacks a nationally-coordinated program designed to attract a greater percentage of world travel. Canada, for instance, invests $80 million per year on its national marketing program, and Australia invests more than $100 million. Even New Zealand, a country 1/74th the size of the U.S., invests $43 million each year promoting itself to world travelers.

The absence of a nationally-coordinated campaign that communicates the common qualities of U.S. destinations represents a significant competitive disadvantage.

Other countries use nationally-coordinated programs to formulate consistent, compelling messages with proper timing to ensure maximum effectiveness.

While some individual destinations and private sector businesses from the U.S. currently invest in marketing internationally, the absence of a nationally-coordinated umbrella campaign that communicates the common qualities of these destinations represents a significant competitive disadvantage for the U.S.

The potential rewards of implementing such a campaign are manifold:

- **Provide a Coordinated Message that Communicates the American Experience:** The power of a unifying organizing principle to better leverage the commonalities of individual brands is a proven axiom of marketing – one that is employed by many of the companies represented on this board. Although a number of individual brands and destinations in the U.S. have the resources to market themselves abroad, these efforts are uncoordinated, conflicting, and fail to communicate the deepest, most universal qualities of the U.S. as a brand. An over-arching, umbrella message is therefore necessary to move the U.S. higher on the list of dream destinations.

- **Benefit all Regions Equally:** A nationally-coordinated campaign will help drive visitation higher in those states and regions that cannot afford to market themselves individually. From the neon glow of Vegas, to the tranquility of the Pacific Northwest, to the music and flavor of the South, to the simple beauty of the plains, to the majesty of the Rocky Mountains, the U.S. tourist experience can be as varied as the imagination, and as affordable or extravagant as one can afford. But unfortunately, without a nationally coordinated program, the vast majority of business and tourist destinations are unable to reach international markets. These destinations will continue to be at a significant disadvantage until a nationally-coordinated program is implemented that can channel visitor interest to other regions of the U.S. beyond the two coasts.

- **Ensure that the U.S. is Top-Of-Mind for World Travelers:** By far the greatest disadvantage posed by our lack of a nationally-coordinated marketing campaign is that the U.S. does not have a vehicle to become "top-of-mind" for travelers as they begin to consider their next vacation or trip. Marketing experts break down the travel planning cycle into separate phases:

  1. <u>Consideration:</u> This phase is all about answering the basic question -- "Where should we go?" Targeting potential visitors with the right mass media, in whatever form, sparks their awareness of the U.S. as a travel destination. This is exactly where a well-executed destination marketing campaign will pay significant dividends.

  2. <u>Planning:</u> At this stage, travelers gather information and narrow down their choices, so the more compelling, entertaining and appealing the information is, the better.

  3. <u>Booking</u>: At this stage, travelers are ready to buy, so tailored, personalized messages should be on hand to help close the deal.

  If the U.S. isn't top-of-mind with potential visitors at phase #1, then the competition will likely be over by phases #2 and #3. These travelers will -- more often than not -- decide to travel elsewhere.

- **Enhance Our National Image:** The image of the U.S. is at an all-time low in many parts of the world – at a time when U.S. reputation matters more than ever. Dollar for dollar, investing in a nationally-coordinated destination marketing campaign is perhaps the most effective vehicle to strengthen the U.S. image in other parts of the world.

  1. **Demonstrate that our Doors are Open and the Welcome Mat is out.** Actions speak louder than words, and the simple act of asking people to visit communicates a powerful message in and of itself – even to those who are not able to accept the invitation. We look forward to the day that people around the world receive such an invitation from the United States.

  2. **Bring Potentially Millions of Additional Visitors to the U.S.** Whether tied to a company or a country, positive word-of-mouth is the most powerful form of marketing. Research conducted in six of the top travel markets to the U.S. – Brazil, Canada, France, Germany, Japan and the UK – established that while 38 percent of those who had never visited the U.S. had a positive image of the U.S., 54 percent of those who had visited viewed the U.S. positively. Likewise, only 61 percent of those who had not visited the U.S. had a positive view of the American people, compared to 72 percent of those who had visited.[37] By giving these visitors a powerful first-hand experience of our values and hospitality, we can create millions of grassroots ambassadors.

  3. **Communicate America's Story to the World Through a Well-Executed Marketing Campaign.** The best marketing campaigns contribute to building a long-

---

[37] Global Market Insite Inc. survey 2005

term brand in addition to selling a product. Many other countries are doing this very effectively, with destination marketing that communicates the values and culture that define them. The U.S. should be in the international marketplace with similar ads that invite the world to experience the land of life, liberty and the pursuit of happiness.

RECOMMENDATIONS OF THE PROMOTION SUBCOMMITTEE

In order to be fully competitive in the world marketplace, the U.S. must implement a nationally coordinated and properly-executed destination marketing campaign. Without such a campaign, the U.S. will remain at a competitive disadvantage in the market for international travelers.

How to best implement such a campaign is a difficult question – one that has challenged both the industry and many in government for years. Resolving this question will require a more extensive period of time, and the input of the entire travel and tourism industry, as well as other stakeholders in government and the private sector.

It is good news that a new effort is underway, called the Discover America Partnership, to do exactly that. This effort led by prominent players throughout the travel and tourism industry is expected to culminate by the beginning of 2007.

In the interim, we are pleased to offer the following recommendations, based upon industry best practices and successful models implemented by states as well as other countries.

1. **Develop a Viable Framework:** Efforts to launch a nationally-coordinated destination marketing campaign have failed in the past partly due to the absence of a viable framework at the front end. We are pleased to see the private sector take the initiative to develop a comprehensive plan via the Discover America Partnership. This Partnership will use the best marketing expertise of the industry, as well as best practices of other nationally coordinated efforts. The framework should contain the elements listed below:

2. **Determine Funding Requirements**: Determine the level of funding necessary to achieve "share of voice" in the top source markets to the U.S. This recommended funding level should be determined through a rigorous market analysis, looking at current spending by competitor destinations, various communications channels, and other features specific to our target markets.

3. **Identify Viable Funding Sources**: A major factor in the failure of past efforts to create a national marketing campaign has been the lack of a viable, long-term funding model. The high return on investment in terms of jobs, tax revenue, and public diplomacy argue for a significant investment by the federal government in promoting the U.S. to international travelers. However, recognizing the historical challenge of obtaining this money through the congressional appropriations process – coupled with the fact that an appropriation may always be reduced or taken away in any given year – we recommend that the government and the industry also explore other approaches to obtaining funding. The industry should take the initiative in this process by canvassing *all* potential sources of funding, both public and private, and also inventory the successful funding models used by other countries as well as states in the U.S., as a precursor to building a consensus behind the most viable funding

mechanism(s) for this effort. We note that in order to build credibility in asking the federal government to partner in this program, the industry should be willing to contribute at least a portion of the funding.

4. **Identify Target Markets:** The framework should identify the top foreign markets of focus based on data gleaned from the situation analysis. In addition to today's top source markets, our target markets should also include emerging markets – particularly in Asia and Eastern Europe – that are likely to rise rapidly over the next 15 years.

5. **Communicate the American Experience:** The framework should identify the most compelling marketing messages, capturing the diverse alternatives available to tourists in the U.S.

6. **Centralize Resources of Federal Government Agencies:** The Federal government can more effectively focus the Tourism Policy Council to bolster more coordinated and centralized promotional activities among member agencies with the private sector, such as the Department of Transportation's Scenic Byways, the Department of Interior's Parks Services and Fish and Wildlife, the Department of Agriculture's Forest Services, and the Advisory Council on Historic Preservation, to name a few.

7. **Integrate both Public and Private Expertise:** The most successful models in other countries rely on a full partnership between government and the private sector. The private sector typically takes the lead on designing and executing the marketing campaign, including messaging, timing and media channels. However, we note that there are also roles that the government is uniquely suited to help fulfill:

   - Marshal Resources of Private Sector: The federal government can act as a galvanizing force to marshal the resources of the private sector travel and tourism industry.
   - Ensure Program Benefits Entire U.S: The federal government is in a unique position to ensure that a nationally coordinated destination marketing program is one that benefits tourist destinations throughout the U.S. – rather than select destinations on the two coasts.
   - Publicize Travel Requirements: The government should also play a key role in helping to publicize issues that cut across different agencies, so that marketing efforts are not marred by confusion and misinformation. For instance, the communication of changes in documentation requirements would require coordination between the Departments of State, Homeland Security and Commerce.
   - Open Doors in Foreign Markets: With its extensive network of consulates, embassies and trade offices, the federal government can help open doors in foreign markets, and contribute on-the-ground resources to supplement communications efforts.

DEMONSTRATE THE VALUE OF TRAVEL AND TOURISM
A Report of the Return on Investment Subcommittee

SITUATION ANALYSIS:

Given the stature of travel and tourism as one of the world's most significant growth industries, it is important that the U.S. have processes in place to measure the success of efforts to compete in this market, in terms of job creation, economic impact, tax revenue and U.S. reputation. The ability to measure these returns on investment is particularly important in order to continue to calibrate a national strategy by calculating return on investment and tracking shifts in the marketplace.

The primary data set for measuring the economic impacts of travel and tourism is published by the Bureau of Economic Analysis (BEA) in its Travel and Tourism Satellite Accounts (TTSA). The data set provides standardized measurements of key economic contributions of travel and tourism (T&T) which can be tracked over time. The BEA satellite accounts, as official government statistical reports, have the additional benefit of being accepted by government agencies and the U.S. Congress.

Summary of the U.S. TTSA from BEA

Based on the information provided by BEA,[38] the U.S. TTSA includes estimates of the following variables:

- Output (or Supply)
- Employment (Jobs)
- Value Added (GDP)

Output and Employment

For output and employment, both direct T&T impact and total (including both direct and indirect) T&T impact are provided. The direct tourism output is defined as the value of goods and services sold directly to visitors. The indirect tourism output relates to the production of the inputs used for the direct output.

As shown in Table 1, according to BEA, the U.S. direct tourism output reached about $520 billion in 2003, which accounted for about 2.6 percent of U.S. total output. The direct tourism output increased about 9 percent in 2004 to $566 billion and 8 percent in 2005 to $611 billion. The U.S. total tourism-related output reached about $906 billion in

---

[38]   Source: U.S. Travel and Tourism Satellite Accounts for 2001-2004, by Peter Kuhbach and Bradlee A. Herauf, June 2005 and BEA News Release, March 20, 2006.

2003, contributing to 4.6 percent of U.S. total output. The total tourism output also increased about 9 percent in 2004 to $987 billion and 8 percent in 2005 to $1,066 billion.

In 2003, according to the BEA, the U.S. direct tourism employment reached about 5.4 million and accounted for 3.9 percent of U.S. total employment. The direct tourism employment increased about 1 percent to about 5.5 million in 2004. The U.S. total tourism-related employment reached more than 7.9 million in 2003, accounted for 5.8 percent of U.S. total employment and increased about 1 percent to about 8 million jobs in 2004.

However, it is worth noting that the these numbers differ significantly from those produced by the widely cited Travel Economic Impact Model, used by the Travel Industry Association, which measures 7.3 million direct travel-generated jobs, and close to 16 million total travel-generated jobs.

Table 1. U.S. TTSA Prepared by BEA

Economic Variables	Units	2003	2004	2005
Output (Supply)				
Total Output	$Billion	19,716		
Direct Tourism Output	$Billion	520	566	611
Share in Total Output	%	2.6		
Total Tourism-Related Output	$Billion	906	987	1,066
Share in Total Output	%	4.6		
Employment (Jobs)				
Total Employment	Thousand	137,520		
Direct Tourism Employment	Thousand	5,416	5,486	
Share in Total Employment	%	3.9		
Total Tourism-Related Employment	Thousand	7,909	8,010	
Share in Total Employment	%	5.8		
Value Added (GDP)				
Total Value Added	$Billion	11,004		
Tourism Value Added	$Billion	285		
Share in Total GDP	%	2.6		

Source: BEA

Value Added

In 2003, the U.S. tourism value added was $285 billion based on the BEA approach, which accounted for about 2.6 percent of total U.S. value added.

Output and Value Added by Industry

The TTSA provided by BEA analyzed the U.S. economy in terms of 26 industries. The industry level tourism output (tourism value added) was estimated by multiplying the industry level total output (total value added) by the tourism ratio (estimated by BEA) of the corresponding industry. As shown in Table 2, the five industries with the highest tourism ratios in the U.S. in 2003 were: scenic and sightseeing transportation (0.97), intercity bus services (0.95), travel arrangement and reservation (0.93), intercity charter bus services (0.82), and air transportation services (0.79).

Table 2. U.S. Output and Value Added by Industry, 2003 ($million)

Industry	Output		Value Added		Tourism Ratio
	Total	Tourism	Total	Tourism	
Traveler accommodations	130,236	95,958	92,677	68,284	0.74
Food and beverage services	413,976	77,548	196,642	36,836	0.19
Air transportation services	109,002	86,512	63,035	50,029	0.79
Rail transportation services	48,320	1,983	28,606	1,174	0.04
Water transportation services	36,352	6,379	14,297	2,509	0.18
Intercity bus services	1,534	1,454	929	881	0.95
Intercity charter bus services	970	792	800	653	0.82
Local bus and other transportation	21,903	2,838	7,656	992	0.13
Taxicab services	11,013	3,449	7,583	2,375	0.31
Scenic and sightseeing transportation	2,303	2,240	1,704	1,657	0.97
			-		
Aotomotive equipment rental and leasing	37,220	21,597	12,953	7,516	0.58
Automotive repair services	107,524	5,968	52,589	2,919	0.06
Parking	10,426	1,640	5,194	817	0.16
Highway tolls	7,781	511	5,958	391	0.07
Travel arrangement and reservation	34,491	32,020	18,514	17,188	0.93
Motion pictures and performing arts	43,013	7,246	17,060	2,874	0.17
Spectator sports	33,104	8,956	23,129	6,257	0.27
Participant sports	41,340	11,090	22,474	6,029	0.27
Gambling	39,991	15,749	22,898	9,018	0.39
All other recreation and entertainment	44,692	12,098	27,185	7,359	0.27
Petroleum refineries	219,524	11,833	31,599	1,703	0.05
Other industries producing nondurable goods	1,884,037	42,274	738,873	16,579	0.02
Wholesale trade and transportation services	1,157,314	19,710	761,352	12,966	0.02
Gasoline service stations	62,207	4,350	50,773	3,550	0.07
Retail trade, excluding gasoline stations	1,070,331	27,171	719,702	18,270	0.03
All other industries	14,147,608	10,857	8,079,863	6,201	0.00
Total	19,716,212	520,000	11,004,045	285,027	0.03

Source: BEA

In 2003, the five industries that generated most of the tourism output were: traveler accommodations (18.5%), air transportation services (16.6%), food and beverage services (14.9%), other industries producing nondurable PCE goods (8.1%), and travel arrangement and reservation (6.2%). The same five industries also accounted for most of the tourism value added in 2003.

Direct and Total Tourism Employment by Industry

The TTSA from BEA also includes both direct tourism employment and total tourism-related employment by industry. As shown in Table 3, the top 5 industries with the highest shares in total direct tourism employment were: food and beverage services (30.2%), traveler accommodations (24.3%), air transportation services (9.5%), retail trade, excluding gasoline stations (6.9%), and travel arrangement and reservation (3.9%). Total tourism-related employment by industry is provided in Table 4.

Table 3. U.S. Employment by Industry, 2003 (Thousand)

Industry	Employment		Tourism Ratio	% in Direct Tourism
	Total	Direct Tourism		
Traveler accommodations	1,782	1,313	0.74	24.3
Food and beverage services	8,704	1,630	0.19	30.2
Air transportation services	647	514	0.79	9.5
Rail transportation services	215	9	0.04	0.2
Water transportation services	159	28	0.18	0.5
Intercity bus services	26	25	0.95	0.5
Intercity charter bus services	25	20	0.82	0.4
Local bus and other transportation	364	47	0.13	0.9
Taxicab services	147	46	0.31	0.9
Scenic and sightseeing transportation	18	18	0.97	0.3
Automotive equipment rental and leasing	179	104	0.58	1.9
Automotive repair services	890	49	0.06	0.9
Parking	81	13	0.16	0.2
Highway tolls	55	4	0.07	0.1
Travel arrangement and reservation	226	210	0.93	3.9
Motion pictures and performing arts	195	33	0.17	0.6
Spectator sports	210	57	0.27	1.1
Participant sports	786	211	0.27	3.9
Gambling	425	167	0.39	3.1
All other recreation and entertainment	452	122	0.27	2.3
Petroleum refineries	74	4	0.05	0.1
Other industries producing nondurable goods	6,878	154	0.02	2.9
Wholesale trade and transportation services	7,265	124	0.02	2.3
Gasoline service stations	664	46	0.07	0.9
Retail trade, excluding gasoline stations	14,759	375	0.03	6.9
All other industries	92,299	71	0.00	1.3
Total	137,520	5,402	0.03	100.0

Source: BEA (June 2005)

Table 4. U.S. Total Tourism-Related Employment by Industry, 2003 (Thousand)

Industry	Direct Tourism Employment	Employment Multiplier	Total Tourism Employment	% in Total Tourism Employment
Traveler accommodations	1,313	1.23	1,616	20.4
Food and beverage services	1,630	1.34	2,180	27.6
Air transportation services	514	1.81	928	11.7
Rail transportation services	9	1.89	17	0.2
Water transportation services	28	3.61	101	1.3
Intercity bus services	25	1.40	35	0.4
Intercity charter bus services	20	1.45	29	0.4
Local bus and other transportation	47	1.45	68	0.9
Taxicab services	46	1.43	66	0.8
Scenic and sightseeing transportation	18	1.39	25	0.3
Automotive equipment rental and leasing	104	2.34	243	3.1
Automotive repair services	49	1.55	76	1.0
Parking	13	2.00	26	0.3
Highway tolls	4	1.50	6	0.1
Travel arrangement and reservation	210	1.53	322	4.1
Motion pictures and performing arts	33	2.15	71	0.9
Spectator sports	57	1.70	97	1.2
Participant sports	211	1.29	272	3.4
Gambling	167	1.43	238	3.0
All other recreation and entertainment	122	1.58	193	2.4
Petroleum refineries	4	3.25	13	0.2
Other industries producing nondurable goods	154	2.90	446	5.6
Wholesale trade and transportation services	124	1.56	194	2.5
Gasoline service stations	46	1.22	56	0.7
Retail trade, excluding gasoline stations	375	1.20	449	5.7
All other industries	71	1.96	139	1.8
Total	5,402	1.46	7,907	100.0

Source: BEA (June 2005)

Current measurements apart from TTSA.

In 2005, the U.S. Department of Commerce funded a promotional program promoting travel to the U.S. from the United Kingdom. As part of the overall program, the Department of Commerce contracted with Longwoods Research to measure the impact of the marketing program.

Individual states and cities also have various marketing accountability measurements in place. Many of these are focused on the domestic travel market; however, some have incorporated programs to estimate the impact of marketing activities in international markets. Hawai'i Tourism Authority, Nevada Commission on Tourism, Mississippi Development Authority, Louisiana Office of Tourism, San Diego Convention & Visitors

Bureau, Greater Philadelphia Tourism Marketing Corporation, and others have marketing research in place which could provide a model for measurement of Federally funded international marketing programs.

The U.S. Department of Commerce Office of Travel and Tourism Industries (OTTI) gathers volumetric and demographic information on inbound visitors to the U.S. through inflight surveys; however, sample sizes are small. Additionally, OTTI obtains a summary of international arrivals to the U.S. by type of travel and residency through analysis of Department of Homeland Security I-94 forms.

The Office of Travel and Tourism Industries also publishes the *Travel Trade Barometer*, based on a qualitative survey (small sample size) designed to collect input from active travel trade professionals selling travel to the U.S. The *Barometer* provides general forecasts of trends and demand 3-6 months out.

Statistics Canada provides results of their International Travel Survey to the Office of Travel and Tourism on a monthly basis to report Canadian travel to the U.S. A compilation and analysis of these data is published annually in *Canadian Travel to the United States*.

Some foreign governments and operators publish data on numbers and characteristics of outbound travelers, including travelers to the U.S. In Japan, for example, such data are published by the government, travel media (*Travel Journal International*), and JTB Corporation for that market.

GAPS AND DEFICIENCIES:
WHAT NUMBERS ARE WE MISSING?

While the TTSA provides accepted, comprehensive data on the economic impact of tourism, there are gaps and deficiencies in using them exclusively as an accountability measure for tourism promotion programs.

- The BEA estimates of employment generated by travel and tourism differ significantly from the information generated by the Travel Economic Impact Model, which is widely used by the travel industry.
- Given the significant size of the economic contributions of tourism, it will take a significant investment in promotion across a range of source markets in order to see the promotional impact of tourism promotion within the overall TTSA accounts. Without significant tourism promotion spending, it would be necessary to isolate TTSA measurements in those markets where promotional spending occurs (and compare those results to the TTSA measurements in non-promotional markets) in order to gauge the impact of tourism promotion based on the TTSA accounts.
- There is a lag in the reporting of TTSA results which limit the usefulness of the data for marketing applications.
- In addition to travel promotion impacts, travel to the U.S. is strongly influenced by other non-marketing variables, including economic conditions, currency rates, restrictive visa policies, terrorist incidents, political disruptions, and airlift among others.

- While there are some measurements of international attitudes toward the U.S. as a country (such as the Pew Report), there are no existing international measurements of consumer intention to travel to the U.S. or consumer attitudes toward the U.S. as an attractive visitor destination. Such measurements would provide a better indicator of the effectiveness of marketing programs than reliance on visitor arrivals or economic impact alone.

RECOMMENDATIONS:

1. Return on investment of marketing campaigns

- The Department of Commerce and/or the Travel and Tourism Advisory Board should complete a review of existing research models measuring the impact of travel promotions. These should include previous USDOC measurements, the Longwoods research conducted to measure the impact of the United Kingdom promotional campaign in 2005, and existing state or city marketing effectiveness research. We urge the Department of Commerce to review the methods used by other countries in order to leverage best practices in this area.
- Based upon a review of existing models, the Department of Commerce should solicit proposals from qualified research companies incorporating best existing practices and their own creative recommendations to measure the impact of travel marketing programs. Ideally, when implemented, such research should include a measurement of promotional areas compared to a control area.
- Funding for future promotional programs should include an allocation for effectiveness research.

2. Travel and tourism industry's contributions to economy and job creation

- The BEA Travel and Tourism Satellite Accounts estimates differ from those produced by the Travel Industry Association of America (TIA) through its Travel Economic Impact Model using a different methodology. TIA has been working closely with the BEA and OTTI to reconcile these differences and to improve our national statistics for the U.S. travel and tourism industry. We support and recommend that this work be continued.
- Specific metrics within TTSAs should be identified and consistently reported to opinion leaders and stakeholders. Prospective tracking measurements from the TTSA could include:
  - Direct tourism output
  - Total tourism-related output
  - Direct tourism employment
  - Total tourism-related employment
  - Tourism value added GDP
  - Tourism share of total GDP

3. Perceptions of U.S. among international travelers

- With the adoption of recommendation 1 (measuring return on investment for marketing campaigns), it is possible to design research to measure intention to travel and attitudes toward the U.S. as a travel destination. Unlike the Pew Report (which measures overall attitudes about the U.S.) research can be tailored to specifically measure factors related to travel. Specifically:
  - Respondents can be screened so that the sample is composed of potential international travelers (rather than the population at large).
  - With tracking research fielded in multiple markets, shifts in perceptions can be measured both against a base and against a control in order to ascertain the impact of promotional programs.
- As noted earlier, a review of existing research models from states and other countries, and the solicitation of research proposals through a request for proposals can provide creative input to develop an effective measurement system for travel attitudes and intentions.

4. Support for permanent funding.

- The implementation of a program to measure marketing effectiveness and track a return on investment should be used as an integral support point for permanent, dedicated funding for tourism promotion.

U.S. TTAB MEMBER ROSTER

Chairman

Mr. James Rasulo, Chairman, Walt Disney Parks and Resorts

Vice-Chair

Ms. Marilyn Carlson Nelson, Chairman and CEO, Carlson Companies, Inc.

Board Members

Mr. Charles Gargano, Chairman and CEO, Empire State Development Corporation

Ms. Noel Irwin Hentschel, Chairman, Co-Founder and CEO, AmericanTours International

Mr. Jeremy M. Jacobs, Sr., Chairman and CEO, Delaware North Companies, Inc.

Mr. Rex D. Johnson, President and CEO, Hawaii Tourism Authority

Mr. Lawrence K. Katz, President and CEO, Dot's Diner Restaurant Chain

Mr. Jonathan Linen, Vice Chairman, American Express Company

Mr. J. W. Marriott, Jr., Chairman and CEO, Marriott International, Inc.

Mr. Manuel Stamatakis , Chairman of the Board, The Greater Philadelphia Tourism Marketing Corporation

Mr. Robert S. Taubman, Chairman, President & CEO, The Taubman Centers, Inc.

Mr. Andrew C. Taylor, Chairman and CEO, Enterprise Rent-A-Car

Mr. Glenn F. Tilton, Chairman, President, CEO, United Airlines

Mr. Jonathan M. Tisch, Chairman and CEO, Loews Hotels

Ex-Officio Members

Mr. Mike Fullerton, Deputy Executive Director, Department of Homeland Security

Mr. Tony Edson, Deputy Assistant Secretary for Visa Services, Department of State

ABOUT THE TRAVEL AND TOURISM ADVISORY BOARD

The U.S. Travel and Tourism Advisory Board (TTAB) was formed in late 2005 in order to advise U.S. Commerce Secretary Carlos Gutierrez on how to best increase the number of international visitors to the United States and ensure that the share of the country's international receipts continues to grow.

The advisory board is comprised of 14 top industry executives and leaders from across the Unites States. The selected members represent a bipartisan cross-section of the industry. The Board, which reports directly to the Secretary of Commerce, functions as an advisory body, acting within the guidelines set forth by the Federal Advisory Committee Act

At the Board's first meeting in January 2006, Secretary Gutierrez asked the Board to recommend a new national strategy to enhance U.S. competitiveness in the world travel and tourism market. This strategy was to include an assessment of current market trends, the current ability of the U.S. to compete in this market, and a recommended national strategy for the future.

Three subcommittees were formed in order to carry out this work:

Promotion Subcommittee:

This subcommittee is charged with examining the factors critical to a successful implementation of a long term destination marketing program, including necessary funding levels; source of funding; administration; government and private sector involvement; and target markets. This subcommittee also provides advice on the implementation of current government international tourism promotion activities.

> **Chair:**   **Andrew Taylor, Enterprise Rent-A-Car**
> Charles Gargano, Empire State Development Corporation
> Robert Taubman, The Taubman Centers, Inc.
> Manny Stamatakis, The Greater Philadelphia Tourism Marketing Corporation
> J.W. Marriott, Marriott International, Inc.
> Jay Rasulo, Walt Disney Parks and Resorts

Ease of Travel and Public Diplomacy Subcommittee:

This subcommittee is charged with recommending improvements in government policy to improve ease of travel and enhance the worldwide image of the United States. Issues include providing policy considerations regarding entry/exit procedures for the United States, barriers to air travel, taxation, and government regulations. This subcommittee also is charged with recommending ways that the industry can partner with the State Department on improving the U.S. image around the world.

Chair: **Glenn F. Tilton,** United Airlines
Jeremy Jacobs, Delaware North Companies, Inc.
J.W. Marriott, Marriott International, Inc.
Andrew Taylor, Enterprise Rent-A-Car
Jonathan Tisch, Loews Hotels
Jay Rasulo, Walt Disney Parks and Resorts
Marilyn Carlson-Nelson, Carlson Companies, Inc
Jonathan Linen, American Express Company
Noel Irwin Hentschel, AmericanTours International

Return on Investment:

This subcommittee is charged with recommending national standards to measure the impact of the industry on the economy, balance of trade, job creation travel trends, and market segments. The subcommittee will examine the current set of studies and programs performed by DOC and the industry (including travel and tourism satellite accounts and impact studies) and recommend additional forms of measurement as needed.

Chair: **Rex Johnson, Hawaii Tourism Authority**
Manny Stamatakis, The Greater Philadelphia Tourism Marketing Corporation
Jonathan Linen, American Express Company
Larry Katz, Dot's Diner Restaurant Chain